MINI-SAGAS
1999

MINI-SAGAS 1999

FROM
𝕿𝖍𝖊 𝕯𝖆𝖎𝖑𝖞 𝕿𝖊𝖑𝖊𝖌𝖗𝖆𝖕𝖍

MINI-SAGA COMPETITION 1999

devised and edited by
BRIAN ALDISS

in support of the
ARVON FOUNDATION

with sponsorship from the
JERWOOD CHARITABLE FOUNDATION

SUTTON PUBLISHING

First published in 1999 by
Sutton Publishing Limited · Phoenix Mill
Thrupp · Stroud · Gloucestershire · GL5 2BU

British Library Cataloguing in Publication Data
A catalogue record for this book is available from the British Library.

ISBN 0-7509-2360-1

Typeset in 13/18 pt Baskerville.
Typesetting and origination by
Sutton Publishing Limited.
Printed in Great Britain by
Biddles, Guildford, Surrey.

Contents

Foreword

John Humphrys

It is both a curse and a blessing that if you appear regularly on television or radio you are deemed a 'personality' and thus are invited to perform assorted public functions: chairing debates, addressing sixth form colleges, opening fêtes, judging competitions. That last is the real killer. I once agreed, during an exceptionally busy few months, to judge a competition for the best television documentaries. My condition was that the winnowing process would leave me with no more than the minimum of programmes to view. The organisers promised . . . and then sent to my office a box of video cassettes so bulky it took two strong young producers to carry it to the car. There goes another weekend. Never again, I said. And then I was asked to judge the mini-sagas.

The same promise was made and, this time, honoured. But with the best winnowing in the world you are still left with an awful lot to read when there are nine thousand entries. Now here's the thing that surprised me: the reading was a joy. I had expected to be climbing the walls after the first few hundred and throwing myself off the roof by the time I was into four figures but not so.

True, after the first few hundred you detect recurring patterns and styles. You spot the artifice in arriving at what is meant to be the surprising climax. You wince at some of the clumsier devices to save a word here or a phrase there. And there is always the problem, much commented on by the great Brian Aldiss, of the titles. Call me finicky, but I personally draw the line at the title having nearly as many words as the story itself. But when I finally put the last one aside I found myself wanting more.

Perhaps mini-sagas are like Chinese meals; you're still hungry after you've eaten the lot. Or perhaps they are simply addictive, like salted peanuts, and you can't stop dipping your hand in the bowl. Or perhaps each one of them holds the promise that this will be *the* defining mini-saga, the Holy Grail we have sought so long.

No matter if you do not find your personal treasure among this collection. I guarantee that you will be entertained, amused, stimulated, moved, and even encouraged to have a go yourself next time around if you have not already.

No, I did not enter my own fifty words. But next time . . . well, I have picked up one or two ideas, and it can't possibly be more difficult than trying to conduct an intelligent interview with a politician in four minutes. Can it?

Introduction

Brian Aldiss

This time round, in our fifth *Daily Telegraph* mini-sagas competition, we received something like nine thousand entries. Clearly the country is not in too bad shape! And clearly anyone can write a story of no more than fifty words.

Or can they? The rules are simple. A mini-saga consists of fifty words, neither more nor less. Hyphenated words may count as one or two, at the competitor's discretion. And the title must not be more than fifteen words long. But . . .

Well, for instance, a prosy title can spoil a good story. 'How Mrs Hubbard Managed to Fit into an Overlarge Cupboard, with Her Dog' tells us too much. 'The Cupboard Problem' is a better label, because more concise. Brevity is the soul of wit, and a mini-saga (a *brian*?) is the soul of brevity.

Sometimes concision adds mystery to the tale. We can illustrate this with a mini-saga:

The Short Life of Rosetta Stone

I couldn't understand this mini-saga. Has Rosetta Stone remarried? Or was the dark man her doctor?

I gave it a shake. Oh, I see, the dark man is a bigamist. In which case . . .

Another gentle shake. Ha! That couple were her parents.

So much life crammed into fifty words! Admirable!

Well, a mini-saga is a minor art form, but those who find themselves in this anthology have reason to be pleased with themselves – if only for fifty minutes.

The judges this year were Maggie Gee, the novelist, Imogen Stubbs, the actress, John Humphrys, the spirit of BBC Radio 4's *Today*, Tom Payne, assistant literary editor of *The Daily Telegraph*, and me. Our referee was David Pease, director of the Arvon Foundation.

The mini-sagas collected in this anthology comprise the five prize-winners, ten winners of book tokens, fifteen offerings by the famous and invited, which have already been published in the paper, plus almost two hundred others selected by the judges – though there too one discovers famous names, such as Rachel Billington and Brian Patten.

We observed that a higher percentage of contributors than ever were women, bursting in gleefully with their men and drink problems. It may have been a coincidence that many stories featured wives killing off unsatisfactory husbands. Several stories began with the offending male already buried under the patio.

Rather too many biters were bitten for my taste. There were fewer entries in what, last time round, we termed 'The Fabulous'. And none about the EU or international relations. Is the EU too grave a matter for fifty words?

The Hot Air Balloon

Tony Blair, Gerhardt Schroeder, and other EU leaders ascended in a hot air balloon.

They didn't enjoy the trip. An air current reminded them of the currency problem.

When a bird punctured the fabric, 'Was it an emu?', quipped Blair.

They were sinking over Brussels. 'Breathe harder, everyone!', called Schroeder.

No. No, it certainly isn't easy. Let's try again.

The Dragon Slayers

Grandson Thomas was playing with a friend.

'We're killing dragons!'

Their play became more violent. Dragons were bleeding and dying everywhere, to boyish laughter.

'This dragon we'll crush in a dustbin! Bang! Bang!!'

Alarmed, I protested. 'The Chinese like dragons. They think dragons are good.'

'But we're Americans!', they shouted.

Personal relationships predominated this year. There were fewer stories about dinosaurs, but more set in overseas venues – and more contributors living overseas. Considering that we are supposedly a post-Christian society, we noticed that Adam and Eve still held a place in the popularity stakes (perhaps because they make an ideal pair for quarrels?). Other famous people mentioned, at least in passing, include Anna Ford, Marlene Dietrich, Friedrich Nietzsche and Alan Titchmarsh – perhaps some indication of *Telegraph* readers' interests. God featured quite largely, although one could not but feel his name was often taken in vain, if not humorous vein.

Many thanks to all who took part. Never think that a mere fifty words can cramp your style. You would find, if a mini-saga ran to one hundred words, that the game would be twice as hard.

Love
&
Hate

TWILIGHT

Exhausted by his jealousy, she said, 'Promise you won't open this letter for an hour. If you do, I'll leave you forever.'

He was tormented as to where she was going, but still he promised.

Immediately she left he opened the letter. It read, 'I am returning in three minutes.'

BRIAN PATTEN

LONDON W14

THE SNIPER

He had countless affairs, involving usually his friends' wives.

She blamed *them*; the husbands reproached themselves.

They whisked their wives away; he returned.

A regular pattern.

Nearing retirement, she relaxed.

He had a final fling with a floozie whose husband threw her out.

They went off together.

She blamed herself.

ANNE STREVENS

EPSOM

A FAMILY AFFAIR

'I do' said the bride.

'I always will' said he, but glanced back as he spoke at the woman behind.

Only the woman's son noticed the look between the bride's sister and the bridegroom.

His view of intimate relationships altered from that moment.

And he loved his father more.

LEONIE MERRIFIELD

MARK

ONE IN THE MORNING

'Thanks for making everything so unpleasant.'

She was dressing, the curve of her back smooth with moonlight, familiar.

She was all familiar: bitten into his thought.

'Thanks for . . . ?' He could hear himself sounding stupid, nakedly failed. He reached for her, 'Please, I don't know how to do this.' – touched nothing.

A.L. KENNEDY

COMMISSIONED STORY

TRUE LOVE

Raven-haired Ida had her winning ways. Husband Martin adored her.

Nevertheless, she insulted him, sulked, took lovers, enjoyed awful pop music, drank too much.

Martin kept quiet about all that.

'You're perfect, darling!', he said, when she cried in self-reproach.

She died. He continued to love her, and to mourn.

NICKY BURNET
HOCKLEY

HOW TO PICK UP GIRLS AT BUS-STOPS

'I have an incurable illness,' the young man said, 'and only a short time to live.'

The girl at the bus-stop looked concerned.

'Oh, it's quite common,' he said, 'but it's not contagious, though the effects are global.'

He took her in his arms and kissed her.

'It's called mortality.'

DAVID ALLEN

MANCHESTER

WHO'S WHO

When ten-year-old Owen asked his father
what progenitor meant, Euwan, drunk and
expansive, replied: 'You are my progeny, son.
I am your progenitor.'

Glenys, his dissatisfied wife of fifteen years,
took issue, but Euwan mocked her. 'English
was never your strong point.'

'No. But Jones the baker was.'

NICOLA HARRISON

SHEFFIELD

SISTERLY LOVE

'She can't stay with us,' he snapped.

'But she's my sister,' his wife pleaded. 'She's devastated by her divorce. We must help her.'

Time passes.

'She can't stay with us,' he said desperately.

'But she's my sister,' she replied, tormented.

'She's my wife,' he said, 'but I love you.'

SHANNON SAVVAS

CHATHAM

GOOD NEWS FOR SOME

I brought the good news home. There was a note.

'I've left you. Fed up with your failure. Jim's a go-getter. Now he's got me.'

I phoned Jill. 'Good news, darling! I've been promoted. Better news! Betty's left me for Jim. Best news! Now Jim's got to work under me.'

GEOFFREY RICHARDS

HINDON

SIX FEET UNDER

Mother was dying when she met the love of my life.

'Dirty shoes,' she sighed.

'Don't let him get his feet under the table.'

'Dementia,' said my sister and wept when mum missed my wedding.

Suddenly our six-year-old squeals beneath the tablecloth:

'Daddy's foot is on Auntie's leg!'

LOUISE OLIVER

HEBDEN BRIDGE

RUNNER-UP

WANTED: THE WILDERNESS!

I love a distant Canadian lady who once said jokingly that black bears invade her garden. She teased me for believing.

'Fallston is too suburban for bears,' said she.

Now she sends me cards depicting bears.

So she too wanted to believe.

Bears or suburbs: which moves the imagination more?

BRIAN ALDISS

COMMISSIONED STORY

THERE ARE ALWAYS OTHER SENSES

An icy accident deafened and embittered him.

Summer flowers and a pretty florist overcame him. Too shy to buy, he left her love-notes impaled upon stolen roses. When fingertips brushed (happy chance), he blushed and tried out his lost voice shamefacedly. 'I'm deaf you fool!' she wrote, smiling.

Love blossomed.

KATIE AMBLER
LONDON SW4

SCREEN IDOL

Women everywhere adore me, a love-god in their dreams.

But off-screen, off my pedestal, I'm alone again, my glamorous third wife's lawyers claiming millions. Yet once she dreamed of love with me.

I too dream, not of beautiful love-goddesses, but of some simple girl who's just as short as me.

ROLAND KIRTLEY

BARNSTAPLE

HIGHLY COMMENDED

TARGET OF AFFECTION

She left without saying where she was going.
It wasn't the first time. Her husband followed
her, parking some distance from where she
met her lover.

The husband's rifle failed to hit its target.
He scurried home.

On her return the wife innocently shouted,
'Missed me?'

'Yes,' seethed the husband.

ALEXANDER COTTON

LONDON SE1

THE MOGUL AND THE STARLET

He spotted her talents in a box-office flop.
She yielded to furs, flattery and the
mandatory couch imbroglio.
    His technique was perfunctory.
    'Ouch!' she said.

After glitzy nuptials, a spoilt brat and a few
B movies, his interest strayed. Her technique
was exemplary; she settled for millions.
    'Ouch!' he said.

GUY CARTER
LONDON E17

A MOTHER'S LOVE

Mother was freshly buried. My icy fingers clutched her fur tightly around me; even now she seemed to resent the offering of protection.

An expensive button sprang off, tinking and coining its way along the stones.

'Is this really yours?' my husband enquired. Her lover's cold blue eyes searched mine.

PAMELA MANN
HARPENDEN

OF VIRGINS AND UNICORNS

They laughed behind her back, called her dried-up old spinster. One day she went to the forest; they followed giggling. She sat in a sun-lit glade, let down her hair and called. The unicorn came on dainty silver hooves, laid his head in her lap. They stopped laughing.

JENNIFER SHORTMAN

YATTON

CLOSER ACQUAINTANCE

At first she thought him an arrogant, ruthless bastard. But when he began to pay attention to her, she was charmed. He was nice when you knew him, she realised.

They married. He wasn't fair to her. She complained. He left her. Now she thinks him an arrogant, ruthless bastard.

WENDY COPE

COMMISSIONED STORY

WAR AND PIECES

'Edge pieces first,' he decrees.
All others are rounded up, segregated.
'Blues into the blue pile, browns into the
brown. Do not mix them.'
My moves are restricted (a tree here,
a cloud there), while he attacks the castle.
I smuggle a piece into my pocket: the
revolution has begun.

MARY ANN SLATER
LONDON SW7

FIRST PRIZE

MIND THE GAP

'What I really want is to take a year off.'

'Off what?' he replied incredulously.

'Just off – everything.' She shrugged her shoulders.

'You can't do any such thing. You've got responsibilities. What about me and the children?'

'I know. That is the point. I want to take a year off.'

HILARY M. WALLACE

KEMPSEY

PRIVATE VIEWING

She swam into the party on a dry martini.
He stood straight as a straw. She tried to
break the ice but left only a chip on his
shoulder. He sold only one damn painting
that night. Of her, of course – it paid for the
divorce. He got the cat.

GLENDA RICHARDS

LONDON SW9

Home
&
Abroad

BREAKING LINKS

When she saw both cars snuggled in Sandra's driveway, side by side, it hit her. 'You're having an affair.'

Her beloved husband confessed, apologised.

It was over.

The image of those two conspiratorial rear numberplates haunted her constantly.

'What can I do?' he asked regretfully.

'Change your car,' Felicity said.

LORNA DAYMOND

WYMONDHAM

AN ESCAPE

A girl who walked through Regent's Park to school felt compelled to place offerings of sweets, or cake, at the feet of a statue of a beautiful young woman, 'A Defender of the Helpless'. One day someone put near yesterday's bird-pecked biscuit a booklet on the language of flowers.

DORIS LESSING

COMMISSIONED STORY

THE OLD HOUSE

Our dear old house! Five generations of our family lived there. Every room has a history.

I'm the last of the line – 'Old mad Molly', they call me. Maybe, but poverty . . .

I sold out to a rich Arab.

'I will care for your house, ma'am,' he said.

But that minaret . . .

PEGGY WILSON

HASTINGS

THE VERY SUCCESSFUL SOLICITOR WHO LIVED IN THE BIGGEST HOUSE IN TOWN

His children were expensive and so was his wife. Prison for a solicitor is bad for business, but that doesn't excuse child abuse. Especially not with his eldest daughter. No one had guessed a thing. His clothes were found on the pier. Everyone wondered who'd buy the big house next.

RACHEL BILLINGTON
LONDON

PLANT LIFE

The plant dominated the small room. Mary doted on it. Her sister's plant had died as her marriage folded. Mary's thrived in a happy family home.

When leaves started to wilt Mary realised he'd been disloyal. Happily she knew the solution to both her problems. Blood and bonemeal finely mixed.

JANE ALEXANDER

CHESTERFIELD

THE NIGHT OF THE MONKEY

The monkey came.

It smoked her fags. Ate her food. Threw up in the sink. Lost her shoes. Drank her booze. Stole her purse. Bought a kebab. Kidnapped some bloke. Re-parked her car. Trashed her room. Swapped her brain for cottonwool.

Next day she swore – she'd never drink again.

CLAIRE EVANS
GODALMING

BURNING AMBITION

Her sullen face was white as salt. Locked in her room as if in jail. Outside the sun was shining. Inside the plain, dull room seemed to close in on her. She wanted to fill it with light, with colour. She wanted excitement.

The girl struck the match and smiled.

Michelle Basquill
Aged Twelve
DOLLAR

HIGHLY COMMENDED

TO LIVE AGAIN

I remember my mother.
  I was five when my eyes began to grow
dim.
    River blindness grows fast.
    I grew too and had a little daughter.
    She helped me see.
    One day white men came to our village
and gave me my sight.
    I saw my mother in her face.

CHRISTINE DUNCAN
EXMOUTH

PARADOX IN PADUA

Queuing to touch the tomb of San Antonio, Giuseppe read the letters extolling the Saint's intervention in terrible accidents and illnesses. When leaving he fell down the steps and broke his ankle. 'Thank you, San Antonio,' he wrote later in hospital. 'Without you I would surely have broken my neck.'

DIANA CROOK
LEWES

DEATH AT BERTH

Our landfall, the Brazilian coast at early
dawn. Immediately stevedores swarmed
aboard. In the hour, a talleyman fell to death
in the hold. On deck, under banana leaves
they laid him. Cargo finished they carried
him ashore.

Sailing into the blackness, a wreck buoy's
tolling bell our last sad contact.

R.G. MORRISON
THINGWALL

THE FIRST MAN

'They're coming, they're coming!' cried the scout. Afraid, the people fled to their homes. Except for one man.

The scout ran to him and cried again, 'They're coming, they're coming!' The man smiled and pulled a gun from his pocket. 'Friend,' he said, 'they're already here.'

He shot the scout.

MARTIN BROCKLEBANK

BARROW-IN-FURNESS

TODAY'S POSTCARD FROM MELBOURNE, AUSTRALIA

Outlook Express: One New Message.
   Subject: Dire Straits.
   'Sorry Dad. Rent due on flat; love you
very much; how are the cats?'

My little girl is becoming a woman 12,000
miles away. She worries unnecessarily
thinking she owes me something.
   I send love and more money:
Hotmail.Com and smile.

PHIL EDWARDSON
LEIGHTON BUZZARD

TARTS AND SYMPATHY

The old gentleman had died happy in Gretchen's arms. She was the prettiest girl in Madame's establishment. They searched for identification papers, but could only find some banknotes, fortuitously with his face on them. The King went back to his own country for a State funeral. Gretchen was not invited.

CLAUS VON BÜLOW
LONDON SW7

THE POST-COLONIAL MISTRESS

Anna went to Africa young.

'Embrace me, seductive, suffering continent. I will compensate you for the wrongful rule of my forebears, your colonial masters.'

At last she married Adamu. They soon grew irritable.

'Are you a real woman?' he taunted her, and brought home another wife from his own people.

JANE SABGA

LONDON SW16

A VISIT TO THE OSSUARY IN THE HAMLET OF ST GEORGE, GREECE

I check for the bones of Mr Nikos. Yes, the previous owner of my house is still there.

A misfit, who hanged himself from my kitchen beam.

He was a naive artist. The walls of the house are covered with naked ladies riding tigers: he just couldn't survive life's jungle.

M.A. ILIOPOULOU
LANGTON LONG

THE PRIVATE HELL OF SVETOZAR BERISHA

Father Albanian, mother Serb. Rare, diabolical mix. Draft-dodging, asylum-seeking I fled westward.

Served in bars, washed dishes, floors . . . then CNN showed mother's bus bombed in half.

Father safe; with KLA. Phoned yesterday: 'Come!'

'To kill?' I blanched, allegiance torn. My mother's kin? Or someone in between? 'Let me scrub floors!'

N. JANKOVIC
LONDON SW19

IN THE NIGHT OF DAY

Transylvania Tours Ltd had failed to advise. The vampire snarled, and folded his black silk cloak around him before slamming the coffin lid shut, confined to his hotel room.

   The prospect of leaving his castle for Greenland and lots of unsuspecting Inuit beckoned, but the midnight sun denied any excursion.

R.A. SCAMMELLS

TROWBRIDGE

HUMID NIGHTS IN SOUTHERN CALIFORNIA

My 6'6" neighbour is gardening when
Mother sees him.
   'He's *naked*,' she whispers.
   'He's a nudist,' I whisper back. 'Always
gardens at sunset.'
   Sweat streaks his copper skin: the sky is the
color of pumpkins. Mother looks rattled.
I give her two sherries.
   Within days she's taking walks at sunset.

WENDY HASKETT

ENCINITAS, CALIFORNIA

HIGHLY COMMENDED

THE KOSOVO QUESTION

'Have we forgotten anything?' wondered the Convener, as, through an interpreter, she spoke to the Refugees, smiling, in welcome.

They had refurbished a bungalow. People were very generous.

'No question – everything taken care of!' – She spoke; pleased, welcoming, smiling.

'When we go home?' asked a young girl, in English, – solemnly.

REVD STUART PRYCE

BRIDGE OF ALLAN

AUNTY JANET'S BEST BUY OF '66 AT BAR SAN JORGE

Senora Juanita heard the fishermen had landed a strange catch with black roe. She roared up the port in her old Daf and generously took the lot off their hands at fifty pesetas a kilo. Discerning customers forked out fifty a teaspoon that summer for caviar, fresh from the freezer.

JUDITH HAYTER JOHNSON

SOUTHBOROUGH

LOST AT SEA!

Furious storms! Homeric winds and waves!

The cockleshell boat, *Ulysses II*, was driven into unknown waters.

Before the bows, a mighty figure rose dripping from the depths. Lightning lit its shoulders. Neptune himself!

'Get out of my territory!' he roared.

The skipper shouted back, 'This the way to Grimsby, mate?'

RONNIJ JOHNSON

TOTTENHALL

THE FABLE OF THE HUNGRY WOLVES

The wolves were getting closer as the sleigh fled over the snow. The driver lashed the horse, shouting, 'Shoot one of them – quickly!'

But they caught us.

They ate the horse and took no notice of us.

Men still believe that they are the centre and purpose of the universe.

DENIS SWINNEY

MORPETH

RUINS

The Pipers bought a ruinous old French castle.

Repairs took ten years.

She looked out over the misty winter-bound Dordogne.

'What is my life?', she asked herself.

His question was mute. They stared at one another.

The great shell encompassed them.

It was not horror so much as existential unease.

ALISON SOTKINS

GREAT YARMOUTH

Birds
&
Other
Animals

SEEING IS BELIEVING

'Mummy, Mummy, Mummy. There's a dead albatross in the loo.'

'Christopher, how many times have I told you not to make up silly stories?'

'Daddy, really there is. I've seen them on the Birds programme. David Attenborough says so.'

'Alright, I'll come now.'

'Christopher, that's no albatross, it's a pelican.'

C.A. HARDING-ROLLS
MONMOUTH

FEED THE BIRDS

'Spare some change?' said the youth.

He walked on –

'He'd only spend it on drugs,' he argued.

'Spare some change!' said the mother,
cradling the baby.

He walked on –

'They don't look malnourished to me,' he
reasoned.

He walked on to the park –

And bought bird seed for the pigeons.

Vincent Thomas

TWICKENHAM

ONE IN THE EYE

Every day the Vizier inspected progress on the mechanical bird he had commissioned, offering praise and advice to the silent craftsman.

'Exquisite,' he announced at last, as the bird soared, 'but not lifelike enough.'

The craftsman smiled. The Vizier did not understand why, until he watched the bird's final performance.

BRENDA MURPHY

CHIPPENHAM

TWICE EACH DAY

Beautiful brown eyes seek him; animal
instincts aroused.
Gracefully she waits. This is his time.
Now, his longed-for arrival. Together they
enter the parlour.
Warm hands on her body.
His familiar touches.
Oh, the desired release.
He smiles at her,
Satisfaction,
Exultation,
Joy,
Pride,
His own highest yielding Friesian.

JACKIE MORANT
WELLINGTON

HIGHLY COMMENDED

AN ORDEAL

Strange that the dog should give his emergency bark which normally he reserved for the night-prowling fox.

This was daylight. Out of the car stepped our visitors.

Three days later Emma lay fatally stabbed on the kitchen floor.

They stepped back into their car. The dog leapt with joy.

MURIEL SPARK

COMMISSIONED STORY

THE GIRAFFE WHO STUCK HIS NECK OUT

Once there was a monkey sitting in a tree.

Then a lion came along, he started picking on the monkey.

A giraffe came along, he found a tortoise shell and said evil spirits were inside and whoever was bad will be taken into the shell.

Then the lion fled away.

BRYONY HOPKINS
Aged Eight
YORK

TOO MUCH CHEESE BEFORE BED

Sleep. Dining room, emptied of furniture and completely decorated, contains two Friesian cow corpses. I've examined them. They are definitely dead, decomposing. Smell is awful. No flies yet. Dislike the wallpaper, too flowery, makes room seem smaller.

Alarms ring. Eyes opened. Consciousness brings relief. Still check house for cows though.

SHIRLEY MITCHELL
IPSWICH

AN EYE FOR AN EYE?

Gerald hatcd Maureen's cat enough to kill.
Infuriatingly it ignored the poisoned meat,
sidestepped the falling pot-plant, and refused
to drown.

Gerald did not notice the cat huddled near
the top of the stairs. Maureen found Gerald,
cold, at the bottom.

The cat yawned and slowly closed one eye.

JOYCE WATERS
HAYWARDS HEATH

SUBJECT UNDER DISCUSSION

One fine day, all domestic animals decided to talk.

    'Shall we talk politics?', a sheep enquired.

    'Euthanasia!' shouted a pig.

    'Sex,' suggested a bull.

    'The beauty of feathers,' said a hen.

    'Grazing rights?', asked a horse.

    '*Human cruelty,*' exclaimed a cat.

    'I second that,' growled a dog.

    Carried nem. con.

HONEY MAY HARNESS

LONDON W14

DISCOURAGE WILDLIFE. SAY 'NO' TO THE ENVIRONMENTALISTS

They built a pond.
Frogs and toads spawned happily.
Flowering shrubs brought privacy to birds.
They welcomed butterflies with ice-plants
and lavender.

Wildlife arrived.
Mallards up-ending for tadpoles.
Predatory birds intent on pillage.
An opportunist heron touching down for
breakfast.

'Bugger Wildlife,' they said.
'Let it find its own food.'

PAMELA JAMES
NORTHAMPTON

LIVING DANGEROUSLY.
A SHORT TALE

Her opportunity to sunbathe naked in the rectory garden was just too much to forgo despite the risk of being caught. The warmth of the sun had a soporific effect. Even the passing young curate could not resist the temptation to stroke the smooth sleek body from head to tail.

R.A. NORTH
BUSHEY HEATH

Old Wheel
of
Fortune

COURTSHIP

I am a virgin said the moon to the limetree and of noble rank. So beware my cold smile, my heart is aflame.

And, without waiting for an answer, she threw herself into the latticed branches of the tree.

On the snow, the shadow of an octopus sprang to life.

MARIE-JOSÉ KNIGHT
EXETER

BACKING A WINNER

She wanted an expensive engagement ring.
Three win bets finished second. Two place
bets finished fourth. Confiding in the
bookmaker's blonde assistant, he asked what
to back with the last fifty pounds he'd saved.
It finished last. His fiancée jilted him.
Married to a blonde bookie, he never
gambled again.

ROBIN OAKLEY

COMMISSIONED STORY

A HAIRY STORY

The pavement was crowded. The pushchair wheel slipped off the kerb, the child toppled out, the bus couldn't stop.

Sam dashed in front, put his hands on the bonnet, pushed hard and stopped the bus.

Later, journalists asked him to repeat it. 'Can't,' said Sam, 'I've just had a haircut.'

LIONEL HALL

BATH

A POLITICAL BIOGRAPHY

'No sacrifice is too great for my country,' he declared. The people approved this dedication to their good, and he rose to the highest office. He sacrificed:

His marriage
His children
Several spin-doctors
The Foreign Secretary
The Chancellor
His integrity
His health.
He lost an election. His Party sacrificed him.

ROSEMARY COURT
PONT L'EVEQUE, FRANCE

CIVILISATION

Professor Andrew Clements was eighty when he published his revolutionary theory of history.

'Are we to believe that all civilisations are based on exploitation?' sneered a rival.

'You fool!', shouted another.

Clements smiled sadly. Forty years of hard work and research had bankrupted him. He was civilised – and now victimised.

DENZIL LEAVIS
OXFORD

FIVE HUNDRED REPLIES TO AN ADVERTISEMENT PLACED BY PLAIN JANE IN *THE CUPID'S CHRONICLE*

I'm Jane and I need a man. What do I write in a column for my love? I am small and round, just like my glasses. I wait tables in Clapham and love vindaloo.

'Jane seeks Tarzan to be her King Kong. Petite, outgoing catering professional, who enjoys exotic cuisine.'

HELEN COURTNEY
WATFORD

INVENTION

We had a tumultuous affair.

A few years later someone said he was buried in this house. I bought it, cherished it, a shrine to Élie. The garden became him, I became the gardener. A green thought in a green shade.

His sister visited. She says he is in Calcutta.

G.E. BASTÉ
MENORCA, SPAIN

IT'S AN ILL WIND

He had been drunk, unwise to attempt
reconciliation at the top of the staircase. It
was the dreaded smell she had pushed away.
A death by misadventure verdict let her
inherit their sad home. She sold it for a
market garden, where she prospers, growing
lavender, basil, coriander and dill.

MAGGIE ANDERSON

GLASGOW

BEWARE THE TASTE OF YOUR OWN MEDICINE

He asserted his conjugal rights until his wife grew sick and tired. Finally she declined, following medical advice. He fantasised about having her put down, nagged till her head throbbed.

'Take these,' her GP told her. 'They'll kill the pain.'

The treatment worked.

After the funeral, she married the doctor.

E. SHARPE

EVESHAM

PRIORITIES

'Death is preferable to the loss of one's honour,' she avowed.

'How quaintly old-fashioned,' remarked her friends.

Shortly thereafter she was confronted by a would-be rapist.

'Death before dishonour,' she cried.

'Suit yourself,' he replied, drawing a knife.

'You will regret it.'

'Try me.'

So she shot him.

GUY GOODEY

BLANDFORD FORUM

WHAT IS THE DIFFERENCE?

They drove to where they had first made love, lying in clover, forty years before. Easing their ageing bodies from the car, they smiled at each other.

'Would you do it all again?' she asked.
'Undoubtedly,' he replied. 'And you?'
'Without question,' she answered.
And so they lied together again.

ED TURLEY
WOLSINGHAM

ONE TRAIN OF THOUGHT?

Every weekday morning, for several months, she'd smiled coyly at him from the 'up' platform across the rails.

What madness had possessed him to be on 'her' platform this morning?

She was nowhere to be seen. He'd been incredibly romantic and stupid.

Then he glanced across at the 'down' platform!

NORMAN C. LOCOCK

CALLINGTON

TAKING A CHANCE

Vera answered the advert and agreed to meet
Eric in a country pub.

'Mum, you are gullible,' said Sheena, 'he
could be an axe murderer. I'll stay outside
and keep watch.'

Inside, it was love at first sight for Vera and
Eric, while Sheena was murdered in the car
park.

MARILYN HEGINBOTHAM

OLDHAM

A CLEAN START

It was to be a 'tidy' suicide. Self-hatred made her determined to erase all trace of her existence. She gutted the house, binning everything – cleaning, polishing: scrubbing out the past.

Glancing around, the gleaming brightness sparked a memory of joy. She threw away one last item: her suicide note.

CAROLINE APPLEBY

CANTERBURY

CHAT-UP LINES

Chemistry drew them together across the disco floor.

However, the boy was inexperienced and very shy.

'I don't know what to say to make you come home with me,' he confessed.

To which she knowingly replied: 'It doesn't matter what you say, but we have to talk first.'

GRAHAM BEST

WEST WICKHAM

TO LOVE FOREVER

'I love you,' he said. 'Always.'
  'I know.' She smiled and nodded.
  Time passed. Happiness faded.

  'I love another,' he said.
  'I know.' She frowned a little and nodded.

  One day he returned. 'I made a mistake,'
he said.
  'I know.' She smiled and nodded. 'Too late
now, too late.'

ULLA CORKILL
PEEL

HIS OWN MEDICINE

A waiter lay on a trolley in the operating theatre. His pre-med was wearing off, gowned figures flitted by but no-one even looked at him. After what seemed hours, he grabbed a doctor and said, 'Can someone, at last, attend to me?' Without stopping, the surgeon answered, 'Sorry, not my table.'

FRANCIS RENTOUL
GUILDFORD

Costume.
Dramas

A LITTLE POLISH CAN SAVE YOUR LIFE

In his coma, between life and death, my father saw his mother beckoning him. She was wearing a long black dress and standing in a muddy field. When he pulled through, he explained why he did not join her. The army had taught him always to keep his shoes clean.

RONALD THWAITES

ESHER

SUSAN'S CAST-OFFS

Susan's husband died, leaving lustful letters from 'Charlotte'.

In the charity shop, Susan shoved his suits at a dreary woman.

Dreary? Like Susan?

NO!!

Cosmetic surgery, tattoos, body piercing, clubs, toyboys – then Suzy discarded Susan's cashmere twinsets. The dreary woman bought them for charity.

'Suits you, Charlotte,' said her friends.

MARY WORK

GLASGOW

GETTING REAL AT LAST

'Why does my imagination always inflate things, Father?'

'You're anxious about – something . . .'

'It's so absurd! They say "It's time." I see the gallows waiting. Then I notice something ridiculous, like I'm wearing a pink dress, and realise it's all a dream.'

'William. Pinch yourself. It's time. And – button your dress . . .'

GUY DE CHEMINCREUX

CHELTENHAM

A VISION IN PURPLE AND SCARLET

The new millennium approached. She thought of children . . .

'Harold,' she mused. 'Harry. Young Prince Harry . . .'

'You dream,' said her sister.

'. . . King of Hearts . . .'

'Please . . .'

'I see a William, also. Tall, kingly . . .'

'Who?'

Dangerous years passed. The boys were born all right, and both crowned. They met once only, near Hastings.

J OHN A SHE

CHIPPENHAM

A HUSBAND IS STRUNG ALONG BY A STRING OF PEARLS

Jocasta's lover bought her expensive pearls, which she daren't wear.

At Glyndebourne with her husband, she 'discovered' the necklace lying in the grass; handed it to the police. Months afterwards, unclaimed, it was returned to Jocasta, who expressed astonishment.

Later, she telephoned her lover. 'I'm wearing your pearls,' she breathed.

JANET SLADDEN
WEST WICKHAM

CROSS DRESSER

Naked, snoring, stinking of vomit he lay on their bed. Muttering to herself, she frantically shredded all his clothes into a bin bag. 'Try going out now you drunken slob.'

She left the house.

Walking that night, she met a strange woman lumbering past her wearing an ill-fitting black dress.

MARJORIE SOMERS

LEEDS

HIGHLY COMMENDED

ESCAPE

The fens, stretching endlessly . . .

The old savant splashed onward, exhausted.

The Danes were not far behind. *If he could reach Yarmouth, he would be safe.*

A deep pool lay ahead.

Oh, for a boat!

Or – a time machine to transport him to the civilised world of helicopters!

Fens, Danes, Futurity . . .

CLIVE STAUGHTON

NORFOLK

THE VIRGIN QUEEN – A GLOUCESTERSHIRE LEGEND

The young Princess came riding into Bisley.

She caught measles and in the night she died – bad news for England.

A plan was hatched.

A redheaded boy mounted her horse and rode on to London.

Rumours spread.

'Nonsense,' said the Court. 'Time will prove them wrong.'

Funny she never married.

SYLVIA SIMON RICE
OXFORD

THE LUDDITE'S LAST CONFESSION

They had carried John Booth to the Star Inn.
He had been badly wounded in the
disastrous attack on Rawfolds Mill. The
luddite baiter, Revd Hammond Roberson,
was hovering for a death-bed confession.

'Sir, can you keep a secret?'

'Of course,' answered the clergyman.

'So can I,' replied John.

JOHN A. OLDHAM

HUDDERSFIELD

ANOTHER ULYSSES

Ulysses comes home after a lifetime's
wandering. His old wife, Penelope, has
remarried, and has a beautiful daughter,
Telemacha, whom the warrior soon seduces.
Old Penelope bursts into their love-nest and
kills herself. Telemacha steps over the dead
body, comes towards the appalled hero and
opens her cruel young arms.

SALMAN RUSHDIE

COMMISSIONED STORY

ALLER ET RETOUR, 1685–2000

They shipped John in irons and confiscated his property. Pale Susan, bound in love, sold herself to the crew for passage. His freedom earned, they prospered and begat.

Dark Susan sought peace, changed her town pad for an old cottage by a battlefield, and still pondered roots. John came weekends.

J. BROOKS
TAUNTON

IN MEMORIAM

His great-great-grandfather recalled ancient history.

His great-grandmother did mental arithmetic.

His grandfather used a calculator.

His mother shopped electronically.

He retained information only via technology.

His daughter's memory atrophied.

His grandson's virus destroyed the world-wide web.

Civilisation could not retrieve vital survival skills.

Requiem in pace.

ROSALIND MCCARTHY

COBHAM

THE WAITING GAME

The army of Harald the Hated occupied the high ground. Below them camped the army of Robert the Reviled. For two days they made ready. The third day they did battle and destroyed each other. On the fourth day Simon the Stealthy came out of the forest and was king.

T.H.G. MEGSON

POOL-IN-WHARFDALE

DESCARTES AND THE FLY

Descartes sat thinking. Overhead a fly kept buzzing angrily around him. I am thinking therefore I am, thought Descartes. The fly's persistent buzzing began to irritate Descartes who vainly tried to swat it. The fly had no brain therefore it should not exist. Why am I swatting nothing, he thought.

REVD JIM GASCOIGNE

LONDON N21

A MODERN FABLE

'Peace?' queried the Dove, wistfully. 'War!'
answered the Hawk, firmly. 'From fifty
thousand feet – no losses!' The body bags
came back, filled. Widows and children wept.
'What went wrong?' asked the Dove.
'Nothing,' replied the Hawk. 'Our brave boys
did well.' 'But the bodies . . . ?' The Hawk
shrugged impatiently. 'Friendly Fire!'

B.R. FRANCIS
WELLING

OLAV'S LEGACY

Olav had one ambition: that his children's children might know freedom, even riches.

'Search again, slave. Find my brooch or die.'

Olav returned to where he had washed his Lady's jewels: died for his carelessness.

Twenty generations on, Oliver's metal detector sang in the field where once a stream flowed.

KEITH HORROX

LEYBURN

RUNNER-UP

TYRANNICIDE 1815–1999

We spied his white horse in the distance and a glimpse perhaps of that bicorne hat.

'He's in range, sir, shall we fire?' asked a fellow from our battery.

'Certainly not,' snapped the Duke.

His rebuke wounded us, we stood quietly, children filled with shame.

We never saw him again.

MARTIN AARON
LONDON SW15

HIGHLY COMMENDED

THE FABRIC OF LIFE?

Born on rationed utility sheets, she grew up
in candy stripes and school uniform greys.
She practised law in *haute couture*, marrying
late in cream silk. Children then middle age
incited a fondness for lycra. In retirement she
scorned floral polyester: in death she was
embraced by velvet crematoria curtains.

ANNETTE P. HAMPSHIRE
UPMINSTER

EPHEMERAL FASHION

Young Amanda Potts dressed in the 'Gothic'
style. She wore black boots, a black skirt,
black lipstick and white face make-up.

One balmy afternoon, while walking in the
forest, Old Man Roberts (who used to hunt
game in the Belgian Congo) mistook her for
a zebra and shot her dead.

ROBERT DAVIES
Aged Sixteen
LONDON NW3

God Jokes
&
Mysteries

A QUESTION OF NATIONAL IDENTITY

When the English first arrived in Heaven
   They demanded a dog

God frowned
   The English glowered

God shrugged. OK – He said
   You got a dog
   And the English cheered.

That night, Sirius the Dog Star
   Climbed into the Heavens

And from then onwards
   The English never really trusted
Foreigners again.

BRIAN WALSH

STROUD

EDUCATION ACT

The boy raised his head.

'Sir,' he asked, 'was God alive before or after the big bang?'

'Don't be stupid,' his physics master replied, 'there is no God'.

'Ah,' said the boy, 'was he killed in the explosion?'

There was no response. The teacher continued teaching: the boy stopped learning.

MALCOLM PHILLIPS
TAUNTON

A BRAVE NEW WORLD

He could never get the thing to operate successfully, although she claimed he had tinkered with it since time began.

'It's a disaster!' she railed. 'Abandon it!'

For what seemed like centuries, he hesitated.

Then, sighing, he walked away.

'So next time,' Mother Nature admonished, 'No people!'

'Okay,' sighed God.

SUSIE CORNFIELD
CROYDON

CALLING THE SHOTS

God was busy fashioning His universe, when who should come by but Anna Ford.

Disgruntled, God said, 'I haven't invented you yet!' Ignoring Him, Anna murmured: 'Creation. Now there's a scoop.'

So God made television. 'Can I be on it?' He asked.

Anna reflected, then decided.

'Only after the watershed.'

HILARY LISSENDEN

LONDON SE5

PARADISE REVISITED

Adam had not expected the gate to be open or the apple tree to be withered and fruitless.

'If only the tree had never been there,' said Eve.

'What a world of difference that would have made.'

A solicitous snake slid between them, murmuring 'Try the pears – they're very good.'

MICHAEL LLOYD

BIRMINGHAM

PARADISE NOT LOST (OR HOW THE SMALLEST THINGS CAN CHANGE THE WORLD)

The sun rises over the garden of Eden –
'Boring milk and honey again for breakfast,' said Eve. 'Why not try some forbidden fruit? Old Serpie says they're delicious.'
She picked an apple –
'Do not eat that, dear!' said Adam, snatching it, 'Look! A maggot hole, disgusting!'
He threw it away.

PHYLL BUTLER

EDENBRIDGE

COMPARING NOTES

'It remains my oldest trick,' declared Lucifer, 'to convince men that I do not exist.'

'Yes,' said God, 'I remember that fellow Nietzsche pronouncing me dead. Apparently I had died from my despair for the human condition.'

The two walked in silence for a while before going their separate ways.

RICHARD PEARCE

LONDON SW1

THE CREATION OF WOMAN'S GREATEST ENEMY

On the first day God said, 'Let there be FAT.'
On the second He created chocolate.
On the third He created diets.
On the fourth He created Anorexia.
On the fifth He created rehabilitation.
On the sixth He blamed the media.
And on the seventh He created self-esteem
and retired.

NICOLA REID
Aged Seventeen
LONDON SW16

THE EYE OF THE NEEDLE

A rich man died and asked God, 'How was I?'

God scratched his beard thoughtfully, but made no answer.

'I strove,' the rich man protested. 'I savaged my competitors! I gave millions to charity! Are you saying you've never heard of me?'

God sighed. 'Only from your competitors,' he said.

JOHN LE CARRÉ

COMMISSIONED STORY

SECOND COMING, SECOND GOLGOTHA

The Messiah returned unobtrusively, performing discreet miracles in out-patient clinics. He preached in slum cafés and recruited twelve dead-beat disciples.

'You've got to take your message to the media,' Judas urged Him. He acquiesced and was 'crucified' on Jerry Springer's 'I think I'm Jesus!' programme.

Judas pocketed the agent's fee.

GUY CARTER

LONDON E17

SOME PEOPLE WOULD DO BETTER TO STICK TO THE LOTTERY

She was cleaning the brasses, a job that she detested, when there was a loud crash and a handsome genie materialised, bathed in emerald light.

'Whatever you want,' he boomed. 'No limits.'

'First get rid of this bloody brass,' she cried joyfully. 'And then . . .'

The brasses vanished. So did he.

SHEENA ODLE

TAVISTOCK

AWE-FUL IMPLICATIONS

Exceptionally low tides on the Norfolk coast revealed a sunken cathedral. It made world-wide news.

I, an Anglican bishop, was allowed to enter the ancient structure first.

Pumps were still pumping. Everything dripped. Festooned seaweed caused dim religious light.

At the altar – horror! – nailed to the Cross hung a mermaid!

TIMOTHY SHERIDAN

LARGE SCALE DEATH AND BIRTH

Into the great standing stone
    A magician carved a heart alone.

Storms and centuries soon passed.
    The human race left Planet Earth
    Much like a receding tide.

The sun died.

The standing stone then simulated birth.

Life of stone is slow and vast
    And takes the ages in its stride.

WENDY LODGE

MUNDESLEY

JONES THE UNIQUE

Jones always knew that the 'real' universe was inside his head. His universe was unique. Jones pondered other people's universes but they were a mystery to him. Nothing was precious to Jones, except his loneliness and his dustcart. And when he died the dustcart vanished and was never seen again.

JAMES CORNHILL

BRENTFORD DOCK

LIFETIME

They say that when a man drowns, his whole life flashes before him. They also say that some men seek out that which they fear most.

Thus George became a sailor.

As the sea sucked the ship down George's terror came true.

While he drowned he had nothing worth watching.

JACKIE CURRY

BIDFORD-ON-AVON

OUT OF CONTROL

On the twentieth anniversary of my mother's death I put flowers on her grave. As I was leaving the churchyard I heard her voice say, 'I hope you're wearing your vest.'

I went home, put on loud music and a dress you can see through and telephoned an unsuitable man.

ROSEMARY FITCH

GODALMING

MILLENNIUM

All eyes followed Lady Anne as she passed amongst the revellers, her skirts whispering over the rush-strewn flagstones.

'Who's that?' they leered drunkenly, 'Fantastic costume.'

'A paltry affair,' sighed the Lady and vanished through the centuries-old wall of her bedchamber, her voice floated back, 'every millennium's the same!'

P.E. ANDREWS

MELKSHAM

ESCAPING THE FLIGHT PATH OF REVENGE

Each lonely night Jack brooded over the newscast, willing an airplane to plunge into his ex-wife's house. Or better, a meteorite. Cosmic justice.

But slowly he began to comprehend the odds; it wasn't going to happen. And when a Chinese satellite flamed into a Peruvian mountain, Jack said, 'Close enough.'

JOSEPH NAAS

BRAY, BELGIUM

ULTIMATE FREEDOM

At her mother's funeral she thought,
'Freedom, no more nursing, no more
criticism.'

At her boss's funeral she thought,
'Freedom, no more drudgery, no more
harassment.'

At her lover's funeral she thought
'Freedom, no more sex, no more torment.'

At her own funeral she thought,
'Now I really am free!'

MARGARET O. TURVEY

ELLON

Erotica
&
Riddles

THE PHONE-BOX

He stands staring, nervous, sweating. He gazes upon the exotic beauties who are desperate to make love to him. He knows it's not love, just bought sex. But still; everyone does it – don't they? He wants to answer their prayers, but he changes his mind and calls his wife instead.

ELIZA KEMBLE

THE UNPRINCIPLED FROG. A CASE OF MISTAKEN IDENTITY

He was the ugliest frog in the world.
   She was a Princess and found him enchanting.
   So she carried him into the palace.
   He ate from her plate. Odd?
   He slept on her pillow. Strange!
   She kissed him! Weird!!
   He was unenchanted. Just a very ugly frog.
   She was disenchanted.

ANNE E. SINGLETON
BEDDINGTON

EASILY PERSUADED

'Can I come up?'

   'No, it's our first date.'

   'A quick cup of coffee, then I'll go.'

   'OK then.'

   'Can I stay here tonight?'

   'Only if you sleep on the couch.'

   'Your bed looks big enough for two.'

   'Come on in, but promise to keep to your side.'

   'TRUST ME.'

ANN P. CAULFIELD

WIMBORNE

A SUPERIOR MOVE

My married lover praised marriage.

'Why love me, then?'

'Not to be ordinary.'

'I have a lot to learn,' I tried on his extravagant voice.

'Our time together was extraordinary,' he replied coolly.

When I learnt to become a cool grown-up, I did the extravagant thing and married his son.

LESLEY CHAMBERLAIN

LONDON SW12

SCANDAL!

While hoovering under Father O'Rourke's bed, Mrs Flanagan found a pair of silky, lace-edged panties. 'Disgusting!' she muttered and contacted a Sunday newspaper which headlined: RANDY PRIEST'S SECRET LOVE LIFE.

Appalled, Father O'Rourke, gentle, academic and quite innocent of carnal knowledge, meditated upon human weakness and adjusted his padded bra.

ANN BIDDLE
LUTON

NAKED AMBITION

Hazel Denton distrusted her Swiss au pair.
Bill Denton liked the girl. When Mrs Denton
returned from a stay with her sister and
found a nightdress under her pillow, she left
home. Now Heidi, who bought it specially, is
the new Mrs Denton and sleeps in the nude
as usual.

HELEN SPEED
NEWPORT-ON-TAY

mouse

she drew back the covers and saw three
grains of rice on the sheets where they had
just made love: a haiku on white cotton

    that night as she slept a mouse ran up her
legs and left as dawn broke, gingerly but all
the wiser, through her open mouth . . .

CAROL FULTON

LONDON N4

PRE-EMPTIVE STRIKE

Even Hitler was small once.

My cousin David was going to be the next
Hitler. He made the other boys blow up frogs
and pick on me because of my ears.

I think that is how it starts.

So I pushed him in front of a car and
saved millions.

GRAHAM BEST

WEST WICKHAM

WILLIAM

I invented my brother, William. All through
my lonely childhood, building sandcastles,
practising the piano, riding my pony, I talked
to him. With his prompting, I sailed easily
through school and university. Finally, I saw
him, on the train from Oxford, sitting
opposite me. We knew each other, and
smiled.

LIBBY CALVERT

BAMPTON

HORACE REFLECTS

When I was a boy, people said: 'Horace looks like you, Doris.'

Then . . . yesterday, studying a recent photograph, my wife observed: 'You look like your father there!'

Being now much older than Maurice was when he died forty years ago, I wonder: 'When shall I begin to look like me?'

DAVID L. BROWN
SHEFFIELD

DURING THE NEXT TWO MINUTES YOU ARE FREE TO PRAY SILENTLY FOR ANYONE YOU CHOOSE

Having made this announcement to his congregation, and knowing that some good people will pray only for others, the Reverend Allworthy himself whispers the following words: 'Lord, I pray for all those present who are not now praying for themselves.'

In so doing, does he pray for himself, or not?

ELLIS EVANS
HUDDERSFIELD

DIVORCE

When I was five I used to drive and this is
what happened. 'Why are we going Dad?'
    Dad said 'It is Mum's turn to see you.'
    The next day 'Why are we going Mum?'
    And Mum said, 'It is Dad's turn to see you
now' . . .
    'When is my turn?'

JACK VARVILL
Aged Twelve
OXFORD

MINIMUM FABLE

Piers Fable lived alone in a white studio flat. In everything he did he was carefully measured. Even in the way he spoke. In time he reduced himself to a perfect cube, containing a perfect sphere. His friends admired his achievement – but were sad at how removed he had become.

RALPH FIENNES

YOUR THINGS

I signed beneath your name. A woman in
blue handed me a strangled plastic bag . . .
like rubbish. Somewhere you were cold and
silent while giggling girls pushed tea trolleys
through swing doors. Outside, damp
sparrows chirped lamentations. I threw our
dreams in a dustbin and walked the long way
home.

J. ROBERT HULME

HASLEMERE

THE RIDDLE OF THE UNIVERSE

For their amusement the gods created a puzzle, a miniature universe, on which they placed creatures in their own image. At first it was popular and they visited often, tinkering and making small adjustments.

Gradually they lost interest in their toy and abandoned it, leaving us to our own devices.

G.W. KING
VENTNOR

THE UPRISING

Marlene Dietrich, cool and lovely, playing a
Russian princess, walked down the wide
palace steps to confront a mob. The
Revolution had begun.

I must have been five when I saw that film.

Title? Forgotten!

What happened next?

Only Marlene is remembered, not the ugly
mob.

Ah, one's first erection!

CHARLES NOTIA

ALLOA

MRS MISUNDERSTANDING

Always wrong his wife.
    'He said what?' growled the irate husband.
    'I've got a pretty fanny,' said his wife.
    'I won't have a Doctor saying that to you.'

Evening in the surgery.
    'You said my wife had a pretty fanny.'
    'I said she had acute angina.'
    Always wrong his wife.

CHARLES BERRIDGE

FROME

TIME WARP

The woman pushed her pram along the
path. Her daughter came running to meet
her and peered into the pram, in
amazement. 'Who is she?' she asked warily.
Her mother smiled tenderly. 'This is you
when you were six months old.' Her
daughter just kept staring into her own eyes.

RITA CULLINGFORD

EASTLEIGH

THE HAT

Monday I saw the hat.

Tuesday I tried it on, this way and that, I liked it.

Wednesday I thought about it, was it too young?

Thursday I tried it on again, I could wear it to Church – at Easter.

Friday the store had a sale – I bought the hat.

PATRICIA STRONACH

CHELTENHAM

Arts,
Words
&
Mini-
Sagas

FAMOUS NOVELIST RETURNS TO HER NATIVE TOWN

She had always hated the little town, the dull slow-witted men, the dark and scheming women.

But she went back, and they received her with open arms. There were tour buses in the market-place and Japanese visitors in the souvenir shops.

'You put us on the map,' they said.

ZAHRA FREETH

COLCHESTER

THE PORTRAIT

It was going to have been the masterpiece that future generations would have known him by.

But she hadn't come; that exquisite model with the lively face and the copper curls.

He turned to the elderly grey-haired woman.

'You'll have to sit for me today, mother,' Whistler sighed.

AILSA MOORE
NEWBURGH

WHEN YOU'RE SMILING

A terrific explosion ripped the Louvre apart.

Many masterpieces were destroyed in the act of terrorism.

'Who would profit from such a vile attack?' editorials demanded.

But a small boy ran off with a trophy in his grubby hand. Now over his bed hangs the smile of the Mona Lisa.

CHARLOTTE MAIS

SHEFFIELD

HOT AIR

Feminine charms gained me the token place on the millennium 'World Peace' sponsored balloon.

Shot down over a war zone but luckily multi-lingual I escaped disguised as a refugee counsellor.

A media-celebrity back home, I wrote a best-seller which became a record-breaking Oscar-winning Hollywood saga.

I had finally made it.

BARBARA DAVIES

TENERIFE

THE IMPORTANCE OF WRITING WITHIN ONE'S EXPERIENCE

'Always write from experience,' Jeff used to tell me, over a pint.

Jeff wrote film-scripts about murder, mutilation and revenge; warning me constantly, 'Always write from experience.'

One day, Jeff was found dead, sadistically beaten, in the Thames, with his severed writing hand rammed down his throat.

Me? I write fairy-stories.

JOHN WILLIAMS
BIRMINGHAM

NUNC DIMITTIS

'You can't join; girls' voices are inferior,'
he said.

I will change to Colin, she thought.

The ruse worked. Sunday by Sunday the
changeling was seen carolling among the
boys.

Eventual betrayal led to acceptance of girl
choristers.

'I am leaving,' she said, 'I hate singing
surrounded by inferior voices.'

GEORGINA BROOKS
RAMSBURY

LONELY HEARTS?

Martha found his diary – should she read it? Poring over each page, she gasped with surprise and disbelief.

Champagne in hand, he returned late to find her farewell note.

Celebrating his publishing deal alone, he browsed through the diary, musing on his vivid imagination and his wife's lack of it.

NATALIE SMITH

BRISTOL

FINAL WORDS

Words tumbled out relentlessly, littering the parquet floor. Heavy ones landed with a thud. Light airy ones, those with more vowels, floated upwards forming clouds. Some were colourful, but most were grey.

Finally a particularly long and complex sentence entwined itself around the professor's neck.

He slumped forwards. Silent. Dead.

ELIZABETH BRUCE
LEEDS

CURIOUS DEVELOPMENT

'No matter how hard I try not to, I always cut my subjects' heads off' read the note sent to the police with a photograph of an unidentifiable woman, leaning against a tree. When an enterprising officer enlarged a round object in the undergrowth, they understood exactly what the author meant.

GRAHAM DIX

BIRMINGHAM

MILLIE GETS THE LAST WORD

A throng on the pavement. She sighed.
Another private view!

But there, in the window, 'MILLIE AT THE
GATE *not for sale*'.

'Destroyed thirty years ago, indeed!
Bastard!'

Millie entered, altered a catalogue, thrust
it at the bemused artist; stalked out.

'MILLIE ATE THE GATEAU' Bruno read –
and smiled, remembering.

ANNIE WRIGHT

OXFORD

A TALE OF THREE BUILDINGS

Three porcine architects considered plans and built new dwellings. One used straw – no protection from the huffing and puffing of the local crackling-loving wolf. The second used wood – stronger, but still little hindrance to the lupine slayer. The third found brick perfect; all the wolf blew himself was a stroke.

STEPHEN NEWELL

ROMFORD

WHO SAYS SHE CAN'T WRITE FICTION?

Hating housework the journalist lived in squalor, eating and meeting friends in more salubrious surroundings.

Her books, *How to Run a Home Efficiently*, *Cleaning Your House the Easy Way*, and *Entertaining at Home without Effort*, stayed in the bestseller lists for months, proving that the pen is mightier when bored.

IRENE SWARBRICK

KNUTSFORD

DAILY TELEGRAPH – PERSONAL ADS – 14 MAY 1999 – CONTACT ROYAL OPERA HOUSE

Distraught composer anxious to locate lost opera score of *Jane Eyre*. Briefcase last seen on roof of Volvo at Watford Gap Services. One year's work, one copy only. Due to open at Royal Opera House at Christmas. Substantial reward, two tickets for opening night and large interval drinks if found.

SHEILA COOK

BRAINTREE

McFADDEN'S LAST CV

Fifty exactly. Gone in a breath. He laboured on; condensing, cutting. This was McFadden's final try – the mini-saga of his life.

Fifty. He prayed, and sent it off.

But someone changed the rules.

'Forty's the limit, sorry . . .'

First the days add, then take away. He did not count, at fifty.

MAGGIE GEE

COMMISSIONED STORY

THE MINI-SAGA OBSESSION

She'd got it bad. She couldn't help herself.

She scribbled and scrawled, counted, crossed out, rewrote, started again.

Her husband'd had enough and went away until 23 May.

He returned to find she'd sent over 2,000 entries.

They were broke, overdrawn, in-debt, but still she couldn't stop.

Now, he's suing . . .

SARAH ASKEW
CANTERBURY

ANGELA'S LAST WORD

After searching for weeks Angela finally found them. The sign on the stall read: 'Assorted Local Grown Fresh Words'. Pricey, but no matter; she had to have them.

'I'll take fifty, please.'

He counted them out '. . . 48, 49. Sorry, missus, only 49 left. No, wait up! Here: my last word.'

ERIC HAMBLIN

TAVIRA, PORTUGAL

RICHARDS

Richards wasn't honourable. His mini-saga had 51 words. He sent it anyway, hoping they wouldn't notice. They did. Unabashed, he demanded his fiver back. They refused. He sued. They won, costing him a bundle. Broke, he tried pimping, but his tarts didn't trust him. Desperate, he entered politics and prospered.

TUDOR POLE
WARRINGTON

INSOMNIA

I couldn't sleep. I was restless, tossing and turning. I tried everything – counting sheep, reading, radio, cups of tea. Still no luck, sleep wouldn't come. Then I had a sudden idea. How about writing a mini-saga? Light on, brain stretched, words flowed. I wrote three and slept like a log!

CHARLOTTE BIGG
MADLIENA, MALTA

MINNIE'S AGA – HOW EXECUTIVE WIFE FOUND RURAL IDYLL

Poppy, neglected, seduces best friend's husband, Felix. Friend recuperates with Italian toyboy (great sex). Felix takes Poppy's virginal daughter on guilt-trip. Felix's drug-addict son seeks Cornish refuge with artistic paternal grandmother, Minnie (Poppy's uncle's wartime lover and Poppy's real mother).

Car-crash widow Poppy now bakes prize-winning cakes in Minnie's Aga.

PIPPA UNWIN

SIXPENNY HANDLEY

THE GIFT OF LANGUAGE

A young man with a sheltered background went into the world to realise that his parents had deliberately taught him only fifty words.

Angrily he went back to his parents. 'Why just fifty?' he asked, tears in his eyes.

'You would only have wasted the others,' said his father softly.

JAMES LARK
CHELTENHAM

HIGHLY COMMENDED

THE IMPACT OF POETRY

The poet and his mistress were having a flaming row.

She hit him over the head with a volume of Wordsworth's poetry.

'I wish I were back in Grasmere,' he grunted.

'What's that meant to mean?', she growled.

'Oh, it's called tranquillity recollected in emotion.'

He fended off another blow.

TRISH BUTLER

WOODFORD

Futuristic

SURVIVAL OF THE FITTEST – BUT NOT AS WE KNOW IT

Space bacteria, infinitely adaptable super-survivors, captured by earth's gravity, evolved into sophisticated intelligent creatures. Dominant primates exploited, subdued or exterminated other life forms.

Disease and predation eradicated, over-population, idleness and boredom bred suspicion, enmity and strife.

Bacteriological warfare delivered Armageddon to weak immune systems. Again, bacteria alone inhabit this planet.

DAVID KIRK

STOWMARKET

CLOSE ENCOUNTER

The signals emanated from the clearing ahead. They responded to human transmissions with unearthly alien intelligence.

He moved eagerly, directly to the point of the radio source. This was it – first contact!

But the signals stopped.

No-one ever understood. They didn't check the smear on the sole of his boot.

Paul Munkenbeck

WOKINGHAM

THE FAILED MISSION

He landed the craft silently and unseen.
Quickly he metamorphosed into the shape of
his ancestors, the colonisers of the planet
aeons ago. His mission was to deliver the
message warning of the impending
apocalypse. He paused, adjusting to the
atmosphere. Suddenly he was flattened.
'Bloody cockroaches,' the man said.

SIR HARRY SECOMBE, CBE
GUILDFORD

KILLING WITH KINDNESS

The aliens were deeply moved when they found Earth.

'We must do something at once!' they cried.

It was obvious that the problem was a lack of special paper notes, so they printed trillions and dropped them from flying saucers, whereupon the global economy collapsed.

'Send more aid!' we cried.

GRAHAM BEST
WEST WICKHAM

POCKET MONEY

He selected 'withdrawal' then 'fifty pounds'.

He was taken aback when the machine asked him 'What's it for?'

Thoughtfully he scanned the options, then chose 'birthday present'.

A pause; then another message. 'Transaction unavailable – liar.'

He walked away, confused and angry. Somebody else would be buying the drinks that evening.

JAMES LARK

CHELTENHAM

HURRAH FOR ROCKETS!

An unnoticed fingerprint on equipment is propelled by explosion off the unknown world and passes by planets of endless darkness and ice. It lands, a billion years go by, approximately, and by now fingerprint germs have grown into glorious ice planet heroes. They watch the unknown darkness and wonder why.

CAROLINE KEMBLE
WELLINGTON

CUCKOO IN THE NEST

'We want to order a son,' they said, 'he must be tall, blond and clever.'

'No problem,' said the Gene Doctor.

At sixteen the boy contacted the Child Advocacy Bureau.

'I want tall, blond, clever parents,' he cried. 'Mine are short, fat and stupid!'

'No problem,' said the Advocacy Counsellor.

JUNE MCCORMICK
BRIXHAM

LOVE ON THE NET IS MORE THAN JUST LINE CHARGES

Mike Megabyte e-mailed Roberta Ram, 'Love you.' Roberta e-mailed back, 'Love you too.' They made passionate virtual love in cyberspace but, while Mike dozed, Roberta stole his password, hacked his bank account, downloaded his fortune and then logged off. Now Mike surfs the Internet day and night looking for Roberta.

MIKE RUSSELL

DROITWICH SPA

A TALE OF 1999 OR WINDOWS ON THEIR WORLD

Her boxes arrive.

She puts the computer together.

Hourly at the screen she studies Word, and Excel.

Daily he struggles to shop, cook and iron.

Each evening she surfs the Internet.

Nightly he trawls the clubs.

Week by week they drift apart.

Months later, the marriage founders.

His boxes arrive.

BETH WATKINS

ARUNDEL

DOT COM

We met on the Internet. I wrote forty, single
with money; she wrote young and richly
widowed. Six months of mutual fantasy!
Carried away, we agreed Heathrow one
Sunday. Only our eyes met as we recognised
the nemesis of reality. Addicted, I can be
anyone. We meet at airports mostly.

TIM KENNY
BUDLEIGH SALTERTON

FAMILY DUTIES IN AN OVERCROWDED WORLD

'Farewell,' said Father, swallowing the tranquillizer. 'What's that din?'

'Thirtyniners protesting,' replied Kevin. 'What are old folk coming to? Forty is the legal limit.'

Slipping the Regulation Bag over his father's head, he sealed the neckband, remembering to sign the attached Spare Parts Agreement.

He pitied children of rebel parents.

WALLACE H. BOWDEN

WATERLOOVILLE

Murder
&
Other
Stunts

A GRIPPING YARN

'Was she murdered?'

'Yes, strangled.'

'Where found?'

'Thirteenth fairway, near the bunker.'

'This is a big Golf Club . . . suspects?'

'Naturally. Most members . . . er, knew her. Got my man though!'

'How?'

'The marks on her neck. Used his golf grip! Old Johnson . . .'

'You're a member . . . ?'

'Mm . . . know everybody's game!'

'Splendid, Inspector.'

V.A. GARVEY

TUNBRIDGE WELLS

A BORING STORY

He thought a change of name would make him seem less dull, but as Edwin he was duller than Arthur. From Edwin he switched to Cassius. Nobody nondescript was called Cassius, he reasoned. Then boredom seized him, causing him to smother a prostitute. 'You're a dull sod,' murmured his cellmate.

Paul Bailey

COMMISSIONED STORY

A MAN CANNOT SERVE TWO MISTRESSES

Richard lived for his boat. One Sunday he sailed into The Wash, and was never seen again. Some people claim they see his vessel, the *Nautilust*, on stormy days; but his wife smiled bitterly that Sunday as she burned his dinghy, compass, radio and mobile phone in their secluded garden.

J. TURNER
SPALDING

THE WIFE SHOULD LOVE IT

Crush some cuckoo-pint with buttercup, ivy, henbane and broom. Add black marsh alder and laburnum root. Stir well. Simmer the berries from a Mourning Tree and sprinkle liberally with fly agaric. Serve over privet fruit, meadow saffron and bryony. Pasque-flower oil is optional.

Best served cold, like revenge.

ANDREW HALL
BOURNEMOUTH

PASSIVE EATING

Another TV chef chopped chives and chatted to the invisible drooling audience.

'Golden potatoes and that divine fruit coulis – just setting off the heavy texture of the venison.'

Living alone she became obsessed by cookery programmes.

Her eyes devouring the TV dinners she died of starvation on the lounge floor.

MORAY SANDERS
HASSOCKS

THE LIMITS OF IMMUNITY

Bennie was dead, a hole in his head.

Shot early that day by a friend known as Ray.

Drugs, sex, disunity, 'I still claim immunity.
I'm Consul Ramon so I need not atone.'

The police said, 'Oh no, with murder's not so.

You go straight into jail, without any bail.'

ARTHUR J. JAFFEE

LONDON NW3

AN ITALIAN STORY

His wife believed him when in the warm afternoons he said he needed a breath of air. One such afternoon, returning, he met her – she was out for a breath of air.

'What are you doing here?'

'The same as you.'

Traitors are doubters. He stabbed her to the heart.

Barry Unsworth

THE HOLIDAY OF A LIFETIME

He pushed her too far!

How could she endure the hurt of his repeated affairs any longer?

Always contrite, he would arrange exotic holidays to woo her back to him.

Now, in the beautiful Greek Islands, they stood together on a sunny mountain path.

She pushed him just far enough.

GILLIAN LEY

CROMER

THE NIGHT BEFORE

He awoke. She was gone. At his bedside an empty Scotch bottle. He argued better drunk. Her loss.

Over breakfast he noticed a headline in the morning paper: 'WOMAN FOUND STRANGLED IN DITCH.'

Later, dressing, he could not find his usual tie.

It meant nothing to him at the time.

P.A. DODDS
DARLEY

FENG SHUI

She lived in perfect harmony in the haven of
Feng Shui which she had personally created.

Only *he* spoiled it.

Stunning him temporarily with a glancing
blow from the giant metal wind chime, she
completed the act with the heavy stone turtle,
strategically placed adjacent to the south-
facing door.

CAROL DAVIES
BUCKNELL

THE END OF JEALOUSY

A man lived in a mansion with many versions of himself. A beautiful woman visited and slept with one of the versions. Bereft, the man killed himself.

Another version found the body but did nothing.

Asked why, he replied: 'I trust nothing that happens when I am properly awake.'

KEN FEGRADOE
SURBITON

ALAN TITCHMARSH CHANGED HER LIFE

She dug by torchlight, burying his body where the shed would be.

Years later she remarried. Her new husband loved surprising her.

One morning she woke to find a television crew in her garden.

'We're transforming it,' chortled the presenter. 'That hut will have to go . . .'

'Hang on,' she screamed.

LESLEY FERNANDEZ-ARMESTO
OXFORD

A STRANGE WAY TO GO

'Come, meet my cats,' she invited him. 'I've got twelve.'

Why not, he thought. My girlfriend's left me and she *is* rather bewitching . . .

'Cats come,' she called and twelve flew in on a broomstick.

'All go,' she commanded and he and she and the cats took off into the night.

EILEEN JENKINS
PAIGNTON

FROM RUSSIA WITH LOVE
– A MATRIOSHKA BOX

The wooden doll came apart, of course,
revealing inside another compact version.
Smaller and ever tinier they were disclosed.
The brightness of their colours increased the
apprehension Judy felt as each was
unscrewed and set aside. Finally there was
only a tiny mascara'ed eye. It winked, and
the room exploded.

M.E. WILLIAMS

BRIDGEND

AT TEA-TIME

My friend and I were having tea in our garden, when I noticed two gold-fish wearing collars, standing on their tails at my feet, begging. I told them to return to their pond at once. Obediently they obeyed and were soon swimming happily again.

My friend said 'How strange.'

N.M. HARDEN
SWANSEA

THE BEST LAID SUPERNATURAL SCHEMES . . .

He had booked 'the haunted room' in the dismal hotel hoping that fear would seduce her into his arms.

At dinner he plied her too liberally with wine and exhausted his boring repertoire of ghost stories.

Later she fell sound asleep at once while he lay awake transfixed with terror.

ELUNED M. WILLIAMS
WEMBLEY

HAPPILY EVER AFTER

Doing the dishes, she daydreamed back to the first time she'd met him, before their dreams fell apart, before she learned that you can never change the one you marry, no matter what they promise. Back to when she found him on that lily pad, and gave that fateful kiss.

M.L. WATTS
LONDON N1

PUMPKIN SURPRISE!

It was the day before Hallowe'en. I bought a pumpkin and hollowed out the insides. I cut some eyes and carved an evil grin.

Hallowe'en came. I lit the pumpkin, put it in the window and waited for Hallowe'eners. The doorbell rang.

The pumpkin turned and smiled. 'Trick or treat.'

LINZI ANDREWS
Aged Fourteen
CHESTER-LE-STREET

THAT BLASTED LAW

Devilish bomb this, all wired in the same colour. Red for danger! Now only two wires remained, but which to cut first? He recalled Godber's Law, 'Given a fifty–fifty choice, you have ninety percent chance of getting it wrong.' A pessimistic law which also defied probability!

Reluctantly he chose . . . !

GEOFF GODBER

EVESHAM

NOTICE!

Types of Celestial Transport allotted only on degrees of fidelity: Malcolm gets a Rolls-Royce.

Malcolm had never cheated on Rebecca.

When he died tragically, he felt privileged to travel the immense skies in such luxury and comfort. Others drove BMWs, FIATs and even old tractors.

Then, one day, out of the clouds, he saw his beloved wife approach him . . . riding a rusty old bike.

CRISTINA FIORE-KRASNIC
LONDON W4

AN ON-THE-SPOT INTERVIEW WITH THE FIRST PERSON TO SWIM THE ATLANTIC, UNDERWATER

Passing a towel, I begin:

'Why?'

Goggles removed and welt-framed eyes wincing, he touches it gently to his pallid face.

'Underwater my sadness cannot exist. Silent silver jellyfish bear it away, upwards into the infinite, existence and progress simultaneously confirmed.'

'What now?'

He shrugs wearily, then smiles:

'A bath?'

TOM SHAW

FORD

RUNNER-UP

THE HELPER IN HIGH PLACES

Emily heard the fire engines below and boots clattering up the stairway.

She pushed open the heavy door and carefully manoeuvred the safety barrier.

Surprised and furious she saw a man edging towards her.

'Keep away from me,' she hissed. 'I'm a jumper.'

'It's OK,' he smiled, 'I'm a pusher.'

ROSEMARY MASSEY

WEYMOUTH

THE BIG SURPRISE

Stanley Jesmond returned home from his weekend to find the Garden Makeover team assembled, with cameras, lights and champagne. His wife had described his dream garden, and there it was, where formerly roses flourished: gravel; cacti; bamboo; water-feature.

Stanley's first alteration was a patio; she lies under it.

STELLA D. MOORE

FALMOUTH

Work Places

HIGH-CONCEPT-FEEL-GOOD MOVIE

'Hi, honey, I'm home!' said the man.

She screamed. 'I've never seen you before in my life!!'

He gasped. 'I've never seen this place before in my life!!!'

'Aaarrrggghhh!!!!' they cried, as the killer slime descended.

'Bang!!!!!'

Clint rescued them.

They found true love together in Whitley Bay.

Angels sang.

ALAN PLATER

COMMISSIONED STORY

MR SLADE'S REVELATION THAT FREEDOM IS A STATE OF MIND

Reuben Slade was sick of his routine; same meals, same friends, same old television shows. One day he just upped and left. The East Coast News reported his recapture and return to his high security prison cell in Boston. He said life outside was much the same only more expensive.

MEG MARSDEN

POYNTON

EVALUATION AS ONE GOES THROUGH LIFE

The Teacher set an essay on relations with the Police. 'All cops is bastids,' wrote a boy.

The Teacher was aghast but said nothing to the boy. Contact with the local Police resulted with them throwing a party for the children.

Later the boy wrote: 'All cops is cunning bastids.'

JOHN GRIFFITHS
PENSBY

WHEN 'PERSONNEL' BECOMES 'HUMAN RESOURCES' SOMETHING DIES . . .

Decades of work-devoted days, embracing new technology instead of lovers, Doris nurtured directors and perfected office procedure. The company prospered.

'Someone younger is needed to project our cutting-edge image,' executives decided.

Discarded, Doris meticulously filed her notice, poured strychnine tea for all, and gave the directors the publicity they craved.

L. WALSH
CHEADLE HULME

FOR WANT OF AN HONEST TRAFFIC-WARDEN . . .

Fred parked his car on a yellow line. The warden loved him; she let him off. Her son stole her notebook, and blackmailed them. Fred pushed the boy under a bus, which swerved and hit a gasometer. The explosion deafened us in The Bell. No-one *heard* Time called, Your Honour . . .

GUY DE CHEMINCREUX
CHELTENHAM

FATAL FASCINATION

I wanted that job in the Forensic Pathology
Department.

I asked 'Why did the last secretary leave?'
(without clearing her desk of expensive
perfume – Fatal Fascination, lipstick, new
tights – I wondered curiously).

'She just – went – no forwarding address.'

But in the laboratory, amongst the bottled
specimens, her perfume still lingered . . .

MARY HOGG

SHEFFIELD

SINGLE ISSUE PEOPLE KNOW NO LIMITS

To save the birds they bought the seashore bit by bit, until they owned it all.

Shore access licences were needed, enforced by armed wardens, the Birdmen, who had pitched gun battles with wildfowlers, surfers and fishermen.

Last week Jimmy Thompson was shot whilst paddling.

Now they've started buying the moorland.

R.A. JOHNSON
ANGLESEY

FARMING IS NOT WHAT IT WAS

Bob farmed the land for fifty years then passed it on to Robert.

Robert farmed it until the government stopped all his grants and made it uneconomical.

So he married a cook and took in guests.

That worked, and now Robert lives in the Bahamas having sold his latest hotel.

TREVOR ANGOVE

REDRUTH

BLOOD WILL OUT

Mary, appalled by her dentist's terrible
prognosis, flung herself off the roof.
Amazingly, she flew – joining the pipistrelles
circling the Cathedral Close.

Hungry, and tiring of gnats, she swooped
into the Deanery, 'homing in' on the Dean's
big toe.

Alas! The Chapter was powerless for Bats
are a Protected Species!

E.O.B. KING

DEREHAM

NEVER ASK FOR TOO MUCH – YOU MIGHT GET IT

The neighbouring villages of Hissingdown and Sokehamwell competed fiercely for the title 'Wettest Place in Britain'. They enlisted help from Officials with rain-gauges and notebooks, who muttered about 'Harnessing Resources'.

Now both villages lie at equal depths beneath a reservoir, making the contest a draw. The residents moved somewhere drier.

SIMON HIGGINS

STRATFORD-UPON-AVON

THE ASTRONAUT

Whilst he studied, his friends travelled.

They told him to get out more – see the world.

One day he took off, and saw more of the world than any of them.

They watched the launch on TV and saw him re-enter the atmosphere.

He had been around the world – twice.

L.M. SCAIFE
LYMINGTON

CRUSTACEAN COMPLEMENT

Languid Lionel the lobster
won first prize at Raymond's restaurant.
Ceremoniously scooped from his tank,
given a scalding sauna to celebrate,
put on a plate, prepared to be ate,
he was served to a couple from Colchester.
The other lobsters peered, as Lionel
disappeared;
'and that's *first* prize?', they gasped.

J.E. MESSETER

MARGATE

ALL-CONSUMING HUNGER

She swooped and dived into the house. The curtains tasted good but were gone too soon. It was the wood she craved. She licked it sensuously. Delicious. She engulfed it . . . sucking out all the goodness, savouring the rich essence until nothing remained. She was gone . . . in a puff of smoke.

HELEN SAMUELS

BATH

NEITHER DO ALL ROADS LEAD TO ROME

The surgeon peels off the gloves and removes the mask; dismisses graciously the plaudits of the team.

The way to a man's heart?

The cadaver, still warm, is wheeled quietly from the theatre.

Another long-treasured theory, masterfully debunked once and for all.

Oh, yes. Demonstrably *not* 'through the stomach'.

LESLIE HUBBARD
BAGILLT

JANE GRADUATES WITH FIRST CLASS DEGREE IN MATHEMATICS

In 1980 Jane is first family member to go to University. Jane's parents proudly await the graduation ceremony in 1983. In 1982 Jane, in her second year, is pregnant. Abortion only option.

In 1995 Jane graduates. Her daughter, 13, attends the Open University Graduation Ceremony. So proud of her mum!

CHRIS COOPER

BEDFORD

THE BOOK PRIZE

'I can't, I can't,' she moaned. 'I don't do raunchy.'

'Starve, then,' said the publisher. 'Go away.'

She did. To Tuscany. There, she sat in the sun and typed her socks off.

Now, married to her Italian gardener, she heads the best-seller lists and receives advances hitherto undreamt of.

MARJORIE GREENWOOD
WOKING

SECOND-HAND BOOK STORE

He always said that he could read women. She was like an expensive hardback. Seductively dressed in an eye catching jacket she promised many things. In his hands he found the binding creaked and the pages were well thumbed.

He left her where he found her, back on the shelf.

PAUL SMITH

EARLEY

Life's
Little
Ironies

OUT OF THE SUN

One of the First of the Few –
    He took his Spitfire to the sun – saw
Paradise – the reflection catching his medals.
    Necessity bound him to Earth – the
medals tarnished.
    A new generation went to the Moon;
    They found him at sunset on a park bench,
the Last of the Few.

PAT ALEXANDER

PORTSMOUTH

BEAUTY FUEL

As the angel and the butterfly danced, flowers blossomed and sang of their love. The day wore on. When they tired, the butterfly landed on the angel's tongue. She thought. Was tempted. Then swallowed it whole.

St Peter arrived to watch her dance, and her heart and stomach were a-flutter.

JONATHAN C.M. CLEMENTS

MATLOCK BATH

A SHORT TALK WITH A NOT SO GHOSTLY GHOST

From the tree came a rustling sound and a voice announced, 'I am the Ghost.'

Invited inside I found the human bone furniture uncomfortable.

'You are The Next,' he said when asked what he lived on.

'Sorry,' I said. 'Thought you were a Ghost. Wrong address. Got a Taxi waiting.'

ERIC NEWBY

COMMISSIONED STORY

HYPERTENSION

He hadn't wanted lunch. He knew they
would go mad with the wine. Still, an old
friend passing through.

First course scallops with Chablis 1997,
delicious. 'Another whilst we're waiting,' said
Charles. Two Chambertin with the venison,
Y'Quem with the pudding.

It's the way he would have wanted to go.

A.P. HIGHAM

LONDON SW15

NOT HOW HE THOUGHT IT WOULD BE

'Oh for a few days off,' he sighed towards the end of his busy working life.

He retired. Local organisations benefited. Sweet peas blossomed. Village history came alive. He was archivist here; secretary there; organiser everywhere – allotment, walking, gardening, grandchildren – so busy.

'Oh for a few days off,' he sighed.

DENA STOKES

SOUTHAMPTON

WHO CARES?

Maud got up, drew the curtains and groped her way to the bathroom.

'Carer's late today,' she thought.

Jane finally managed to turn right into Ashley Close, saw the curtains.

'She'll be OK. She can have a bath tomorrow.'

She drove off.

Maud is worried, the water is getting cold.

P. WOODHOUSE
SUTTON

REGRETS

It was windy that day.

Leaves like her brown eyes flew to meet me, catching my breath with their beauty, and lay around my feet.

She walked away, it was merely a gesture of defiance. I shrugged, she'd walked away before, always to return.

I wish I'd called her back.

JOHN FRANCIS

FRAMPTON ON SEVERN

REVEALED

'I abandoned Joan and our baby, Paul, forty years ago. Father forgive me.'

'Go in peace, my son. Your sins are forgiven.'

As the truth was revealed the burden lifted.

Crossing the church-yard, the curate, as usual, glanced towards his mother's grave. An old man stood there, weeping.

ANNETTE BARKER

SIDCUP

EMULATING SIR GALAHAD THESE DAYS REQUIRES A MEASURE OF DISCRETION

Driving a lonely road on a dark night, Clive was suddenly faced with a problem. Should he stop?

She was so grateful. Electrical trouble. No lights. No ignition.

He offered her a lift. Finding a phone box, she called the police.

That's Clive's problem. He doesn't know when to stop.

WALLY NEWBY

SHEERNESS

MORNING BLUES

He woke up and wondered where she was.
Then he remembered – he had gone back to
pick up a bag, and then it snowed, and it
continued to snow and the phone lines were
down. At Motor Lodges all rooms are similar.
She woke up and wondered where he was.

JOHN SIMONSON
WOKING

SAFE MOVES

They sold the studio flat off Marble Arch.

And made enough to buy that stone farm-house near Oxenhope. Both were pleased. No more Martin fixing shelves for the cleavage in flat four, smiled Lisa.

Just clean air, heather and him.

She didn't know they had shelves and breasts in Yorkshire.

NEIL ROLAND

MANCHESTER

PYGMALION IN THE BLACK COUNTRY

Professor Higgins had almost given up. Two months with the Wolverhampton actor had produced only a slight improvement to his client's unyielding accent.

But this week had finally seen some progress. Relaxing momentarily, Higgins admired the thespian's seventies retro neckwear.

'Kipper tie?' he asked.

'Yeh – milk an' throy sugars, playz . . . !'

CHRISTOPHER GOULDING
NEWCASTLE UPON TYNE

TAKEN FOR GRANTED

Jane had been taken for granted as a wife and a mother, until she won the lottery.

She left home, bought a yacht, and travelled the world, making many new men friends. Some demanded considerable financial support.

Eventually, penniless, she returned home.

'Have you been out?' asked the children, casually.

COLIN KEIGHLEY

BROXBOURNE

THE PRICE OF FREEDOM

'I accept,' he whispered.

'Good,' said the General, 'then you are reprieved.'

'Executions begin at dawn, your job is to fit the nooses and push the condemned off the scaffold edge.'

'Will I wear a hood?'

'No,' said the General gently, 'but your father and your brother will be blindfolded.'

K.C. HOLT

BOLTON

SECOND PRIZE

IF I WERE IN YOUR SHOES

Sergeant Boxwell knew he had caught the local burglar at last.

'You don't have to say anything at all,' he told him, 'but your bootprints were found at the scene of eleven burglaries.' Then, triumphantly, 'Have you anything to say?'

'Only this,' replied the suspect. 'Yesterday, I stole those boots.'

M.E. MICHAELSOM
CAMBRIDGE

THE OLD TOWN

'Come with me, darling,' I said. 'It'll be fun!'
  She shook her blonde head.
  Seeing it was hopeless, I went alone.
  My old home town! I had prospered
financially, it failed. Pavements were cracked,
shops closed, houses empty.
  Whereas I was in good shape. But
disenchanted, wretched, and empty too.

MARK ROBERTS

SHEFFIELD

THE CLAIM

Kerkula arrived. He had engaged Neymadeh
at birth, educated her at the Catholic
mission. Demanded her.

Neymadeh glared at the wrinkled man by
the door.

Sister Catherine spoke. 'Neymadeh, the
old man or our Lord?'

'Our Lord,' Neymadeh squealed.

Kerkula caved in.

Sister chortled, 'Nun? Not the first I've
saved.'

ALTHEA MARK-ROMEO
BASEL, SWITZERLAND

PYRRHIC VICTORY

The rage welled up inside him. How could they? Promote her?

Taking a coin from his pocket, he dragged it along the gleaming paintwork. Childish, but satisfying.

She followed him outside. 'Edward. For you.'

Handing him the keys, she pointed to the car and said, 'It's yours now. I insisted.'

NATALIE SMITH

BRISTOL

GIANT FOOTS APPROACHING THE CITY OF LONDON

One quiet Tuesday Mrs Harris was crinkeling her shoegrip on the tarmac when suddenly the day became louder and louder. Mrs Harris said in her mind 'Why is it loud?'

Up above stood a huge giant the size of a hundred skyscrapers. He crushed up houses. But Mrs Harris survived.

J.S. HARRIS
Aged Seven
WINCHESTER

THEY WERE WORRIED ABOUT HER AND, BESIDES, WHAT WOULD THEIR FRIENDS THINK?

Alice was an adventurous child who longed to climb trees. Her parents forbade it.

Alice was a loving wife who longed to drive a Bugatti. Her husband forbade it.

Alice was a lively widow who longed to go ballooning. Her children forbade it.

In heaven, Alice sky-dives with the angels.

LIZ CHAPMAN

HEMEL HEMPSTEAD

HIGHLY COMMENDED

PAIN IN A BOTTLE

'Don't you ever cry?' yelled the bully.

The boy remained silent.

'Empty your pockets, and I mean empty.'

The boy obliged.

'Hanky – ugh! keep that. Chocolate, pen, notebook – ha you're a trainspotter. Seven pounds ten pence – what's in this bottle then?'

'Those are the tears I've cried,' replied the boy.

BETT WAREING
PRESTON

BREAKING POINT

On a Monday he was born. No big deal.
They slapped him until he screamed.
Childhood was tough, adolescence
anguished, jobs scarce. He held on.

His 21st birthday came. No-one
remembered. Mother grumbled – 'wasting
your life'. Tears threatening, he slapped her
until she screamed.

Enough. On a Tuesday he jumped.

JANICE BOOTH

INVERNESS

SHORT-TERM THERAPY

He sank down into a honey-coloured armchair. Between them sat a clock and a box of man-sized tissues.

'How was your childhood?' she asked gently.

'Short,' he replied, looking down.

'In that case,' she said, 'I think we'll leave it there,' and she ushered him towards the door.

BEV THOMAS
LONDON E5

SHELL SHOCK

Peter collected shells. He had set his heart on acquiring the rarest, biggest bi-valve mollusc.

Scouring the world he discovered one off a Pacific atoll – he stroked, fondled, licked, kissed, caressed and embraced it.

It opened its great lips and its bi-valves sucked Peter into its heart.

A conchological consummation.

KENNETH BAKER

COMMISSIONED STORY

ENFORCING THE RULES

The little Fiat was in trouble. The black Audi was gaining, its darkened windows hiding the occupant from view. Tyres squealed. Pedestrians fled.

A small boy was late. 'Kevin!' – a woman's scream.

Impact.

The Audi disappeared into Kevin's pocket as he climbed into bed, smarting. The pursuit would resume tomorrow.

SIMON GUEST

BOURNEMOUTH

THE SOUND OF THE WAVES

The sunlight caught the dancing waves. Ronnie remembered long-past holidays. He bent down to pick up the shell lying on the sand.

'Mum always said to put it to your ear to hear the sea,' he thought.

'It's hard to believe it could still go off,' said the policeman later.

T.J. HARRIS
LONDON SE24

MARGERY

Every Thursday Margery went to play bowls.
Up down, Up down, she walked.

One Thursday someone asked, 'Where's
Margery?'

As they walked Up down, Up down.

'She's died,' said a voice, as they walked
Up down, Up down.

'That's sad,' said another voice and they
walked Up down, Up down.

DOROTHY LOMAS
KILMINGTON

CRIME AND PUNISHMENT

Hearing movement inside the showcase, he rang the taxidermist.

'It's collapsing,' he said, referring to the preserved body of his murdered wife, prettily posed in black lingerie. 'Come quickly!'

Not quick enough. Front door gaping; showcase smashed; occupant gone; his client's eviscerated corpse stuffed with horsehair ripped from the sofa.

R.P. SYKES
SUTTON COLDFIELD

THE HISTORY OF THE WORLD

God made the world and He saw that it was good, at least in the initial stages. But He became increasingly disappointed with Mankind's lack of humanity and pronounced self-destructive tendencies. 'This has been a complete failure,' He complained bitterly.

He ended the experiment impulsively in the Year Two Thousand.

ADRIAN J. RHODES

HALESOWEN

ABOUT THE
ARVON FOUNDATION

The fire i' the flint
Shows not till it be struck.

The Mini-Saga Competition 1999 was organised by the *Daily Telegraph* in association with, and in support of, the Arvon Foundation.

Arvon was the idea of two writers, John Moat and John Fairfax, who in 1968 ran its first writing course. They realised that painters, composers and sculptors all trained by practising their art under the guidance of professionals, but that no such training was available to writers in this country. Arvon was established to provide it.

On an Arvon course, sixteen students, of any age (from sixteen years and upwards, unless the course is devoted to a particular group from school) and from any background, live and work with two professional writers for four-and-a-half days, and write. The course participants must be ready to explore whatever talent they might have. They have to produce, to create. The professional writers set them to work, then work with them. Arvon refers frequently to the Japanese proverb: 'Don't study an art – practise it.' What Arvon courses have always revealed, week after week, is that a large proportion of people possess some talent, given the right conditions for it to reveal itself.

Arvon operates from three houses: Lumb Bank, a large eighteenth-century mill owner's house in a secluded Pennine valley outside Hebden Bridge in West Yorkshire; Moniack Mhor, a converted croft house and extensive stone outbuilding overlooking a commanding Highland landscape, fourteen miles from Inverness in Scotland; and Totleigh Barton, a farmhouse dating from the eleventh century, near Okehampton in the middle of Devon.

Two-thirds of the writing courses are open to the first sixteen people who book on to them. The other courses are organised for schools and colleges, for teachers of English and teacher trainees, and for other specific groups. It is a firmly held principle of the Arvon Foundation that its courses should be accessible to anyone with a serious interest in writing, whatever their financial means, and a Bursary Fund has been established to support those who are unable to afford the full course fee.

Lord Gowrie wrote: 'Arvon's influence on the literary life of the country has been and continues to be immense.'

If you would like further information about the Arvon Foundation and its writing courses, please contact:

> David Pease, National Director
> The Arvon Foundation
> Lumb Bank
> Heptonstall
> Hebden Bridge
> West Yorkshire, HX7 6DF